INFINITE INTELLIGENCE

A VISIONARY GUIDE TO AI'S FUTURE

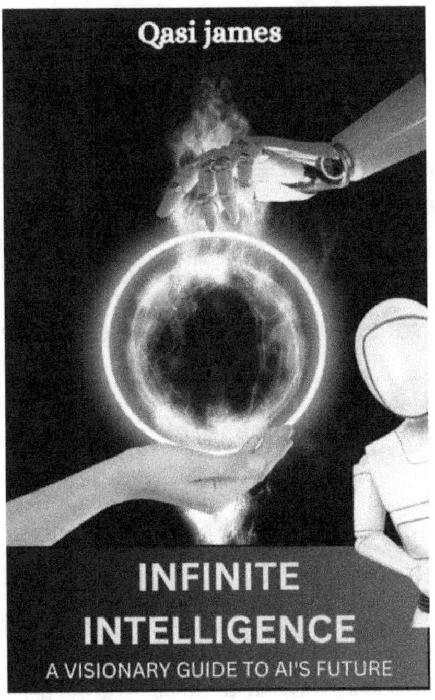

Contents

4

6

Forward

1.1 What Is synthetic aptitude?

At its core, artificial intelligence is the creation of computer systems that can do things that normally require human intelligence. This incorporate a wide range, from critical thinking and figuring out how to insight and language understanding. Symbolic reason and rule-based systems paved the way for the AI era that is currently ruled by machine scholarship and neural networks.

1.2 Authentic Setting

To comprehend the future, we should initially look back at the past. Mythical accounts of artificial beings are where AI got its start in ancient times. Nonetheless, it was only after the mid-twentieth century that the term 'Man-made brainpower' was authored. From the beginning of emblematic man-made intelligence and master frameworks to the coming of AI and the ongoing strength of profound learning, artificial intelligence has gone through a surprising development.

1.3 Meaning of man-made intelligence Later on

The meaning of man-made intelligence in the future couldn't possibly be more significant. It has previously penetrated different parts of our lives, from virtual individual collaborators to suggestion frameworks. As we stand at the intersection of conceivable outcomes, artificial intelligence holds the possibility to alter businesses, address complex cultural difficulties, and expand human capacities. Be that as it may, this groundbreaking power likewise raises moral worries, requiring a smart and capable way to deal with its turn of events and organization.

2. Development of man-made intelligence

2.1 Beginning phases and Emblematic man-made intelligence

The origin of man-made intelligence can be followed to the early endeavors to repeat human thinking utilizing representative rationale. Early man-made intelligence frameworks were rule-put together and depended with respect to unequivocal programming to imitate human insight. Be that as it may, these frameworks confronted impediments in taking care of vulnerability and come up short on capacity to gain from information.

2.2 AI and Brain Organizations

The development of computer based intelligence took a huge turn with the ascent of AI. Rather than express programming, AI calculations empower frameworks to learn examples and pursue choices in light of information. Brain organizations, propelled by the human cerebrum, acquired conspicuousness, prompting leap forwards in picture and discourse acknowledgment. This shift denoted a takeoff from rule-based frameworks to more versatile and information driven approaches.

2.3 Profound Learning and Latest things

The ongoing period is portrayed by the strength of profound learning, a subset of AI that use brain networks with various layers. This approach has powered progressions in regular language handling, PC vision, and complex navigation. The expansion of large information and enhancements in registering power have sped up the capacities of profound learning models, making them instrumental in different applications.

3. The Present status of artificial intelligence

3.1 Applications in Different Businesses

Artificial intelligence has risen above hypothetical structures and tracked down viable applications across assorted ventures. AI is improving processes, increasing efficiency, and opening up new possibilities in industries as diverse as manufacturing, entertainment, healthcare, finance, and finance. In medical services, man-made intelligence supports diagnostics and customized therapy plans, while in finance, it breaks down tremendous datasets for venture systems.

3.2 Ethical Issues and Obstacles

As AI becomes more ingrained in societal frameworks, ethical issues take center stage. Issues of predisposition in calculations, information security, and the possible effect on work bring up issues about the capable turn of events and organization of man-made intelligence. To ensure that the technology benefits humanity without having unintended consequences, it is essential to strike a balance between innovation and ethical considerations.

3.3 Governance and Regulation

Governance and regulation are evolving to keep up with AI's rapid development. Policymakers and industry partners are making progress toward laying out structures that guarantee responsibility, straightforwardness, and the moral utilization of computer based intelligence. Finding some kind of harmony between encouraging development and shielding cultural interests represents a complicated test that requires coordinated effort between states, industry pioneers, and the more extensive local area.

In the resulting segments of this aide, we will dive into ten particular dreams that project the future direction of man-made intelligence. Every vision addresses a feature of the gigantic potential man-made intelligence holds, joined by difficulties that should be explored for a future where man-made intelligence contributes decidedly to society. From the quest for General Man-made consciousness

(AGI) to imagining simulated intelligence as a cooperative power enlarging human capacities, we set out on an excursion into the domains of probability and obligation.

2. Advancement of man-made intelligence: Unwinding the Woven artwork

The development of Man-made reasoning (simulated intelligence) is an entrancing excursion that traverses many years, set apart by perspective changes, leap forwards, and persistent advancement. The evolution of AI reflects the unrelenting pursuit of replicating and enhancing human intelligence from its conceptual beginnings to the current era dominated by machine learning and deep neural networks.

2.1 Beginning phases and Emblematic man-made intelligence

The foundations of man-made intelligence can be followed back to the mid-twentieth century when trailblazers like Alan Turing laid the preparation for the idea of machines copying human insight. Early man-made intelligence frameworks were portrayed by representative rationale and rule-based thinking. These frameworks worked on predefined rules, endeavoring to recreate human dynamic cycles through express programming.

The goal of symbolic AI, also known as "Good Old-Fashioned AI" (GOFAI), was for knowledge to be represented in a structured way with clear rules that defined relationships and decision paths. Despite its success in some areas, symbolic AI struggled to deal with complexity and adapt to dynamic real-world situations. The limits of rule-based frameworks became evident as man-made intelligence analysts looked for more versatile and learning-focused approaches.

2.2 AI and Brain Organizations

The coming of AI addressed a critical change in outlook in the development of computer based intelligence. Instead of depending on express programming, AI calculations engaged frameworks to learn examples and pursue choices in light of information. This shift from rule-based frameworks to information driven approaches established the groundwork for artificial intelligence's capacity to adjust and work on over the long run.

The human brain's structure and function served as inspiration for neural networks, which became a focal point in this evolutionary journey. At first proposed during the 1940s, brain networks acquired restored consideration as processing power expanded, empowering the preparation of additional perplexing models. This approach permitted computer based intelligence frameworks to handle data such that looked like the human cerebrum's interconnected neurons.

2.3 Profound Learning and Latest things

The contemporary time is inseparable from profound learning, a subfield of AI that uses brain networks with numerous layers, frequently alluded to as profound brain organizations. The profundity and intricacy of these organizations empower them to remove many-sided highlights from information, prompting exceptional accomplishments in different spaces.

Profound learning has exhibited unrivaled outcome in undertakings, for example, picture and discourse acknowledgment, normal language handling, and complex direction. The wealth of named information, combined with progressions in equipment like Designs Handling Units (GPUs), has impelled the viability of profound learning models.

The advancement of computer based intelligence is indivisible from the ascent of enormous information. The capacity to handle immense measures of information has turned into a foundation for preparing modern simulated intelligence models. This information driven approach has engaged computer based intelligence frameworks to recognize designs, make forecasts, and upgrade execution across different applications.

A paradigm in which agents learn by interacting with an environment and receiving feedback in the form of rewards or penalties is also one of the current AI trends. This approach has shown guarantee in applications going from game playing to advanced mechanics.

Notwithstanding these headways, challenges continue, including the interpretability of perplexing models, the requirement for huge datasets for preparing, and concerns connected with predisposition and decency in man-made intelligence calculations.

As we explore the powerful scene of simulated intelligence development, it becomes clear that the excursion is nowhere near finished. The following segment of this guide will investigate the present status of computer based intelligence, analyzing its applications across different enterprises, moral contemplations, and the developing scene of guideline and administration. In doing as such, we lay the basis for a top to bottom investigation of ten future dreams that guarantee to shape the direction of simulated intelligence in the years to come.

3. The Present status of computer based intelligence: Exploring the Innovative Boondocks

In the present mechanical scene, Man-made reasoning (man-made intelligence) has changed from hypothetical ideas to functional applications, saturating different enterprises and parts of our day to day routines. This part digs into the multi-layered elements of the present status of artificial intelligence, investigating its assorted applications, moral contemplations, and the developing structures of guideline and administration.

3.1 Uses in a Variety of Industries

AI has moved beyond its theoretical roots to become an essential component of innovation in a variety of industries. From medical care and money to assembling and amusement, artificial intelligence applications are reshaping how assignments are performed, choices are made, and arrangements are contrived.

AI is making a big difference in personalized medicine, diagnosis, and treatment planning in the healthcare industry. Picture acknowledgment calculations dissect clinical pictures, helping with the early discovery of illnesses. Regular Language Handling (NLP) empowers the extraction of significant experiences from tremendous volumes of clinical writing, adding to prove based navigation.

The monetary area saddles the force of simulated intelligence for risk evaluation, misrepresentation discovery, and algorithmic exchanging. AI calculations investigate market patterns, giving significant experiences to speculation procedures. Chat bots controlled by man-made intelligence upgrade client care, working with consistent cooperation's in the banking and monetary industry.

Producing benefits from man-made intelligence driven mechanization, further developing productivity and accuracy. Advanced mechanics and man-made intelligence fueled frameworks smooth out creation processes, adding to better result and diminished functional expenses. Prescient support, empowered by man-made intelligence calculations, limits margin time by recognizing potential hardware disappointments before they happen.

In media outlets, suggestion frameworks influence computer based intelligence to customize content conveyance, improving client experience on streaming stages. Man-made intelligence driven imagination, like generative workmanship and music arrangement, opens new wildernesses in the domain of human-machine coordinated effort.

3.2 Moral Contemplations and Difficulties

The reconciliation of man-made intelligence into different aspects of society delivers moral contemplations that request cautious assessment. As man-made intelligence frameworks pursue choices that influence people and networks, issues like inclination, straightforwardness, and responsibility come to the very front.

AI algorithms' biases, which frequently reflect biases in training data, present a significant obstacle. Whether in employing processes, policing, loaning choices, one-sided calculations can propagate and worsen cultural disparities. Resolving this issue requires progressing endeavors to improve variety in datasets and execute decency mindful AI strategies.

Another ethical concern is the opaqueness of intricate AI models. Interpretable computer based intelligence is significant, particularly in fields like medical services and money, where choices can have significant results. Finding some kind of harmony between the exactness of modern models and the interpretability of their choices stays a test for specialists and experts.

Computer based intelligence's effect on business likewise brings up moral issues. While computer based intelligence driven robotization might prompt work removal in specific areas, it at the same time sets out new open doors and requests for human-computer based intelligence joint effort. Setting up the labor force for the developing position scene is a basic moral thought.

3.3 Guideline and Administration

As computer based intelligence keeps on reshaping society, the requirement for successful guideline and administration becomes principal. Policymakers and industry pioneers are exploring the complicated errand of creating systems that offset development with moral contemplations and cultural prosperity.

Legislatures and global associations are effectively dealing with laying out rules for computer based intelligence improvement and sending. Transparency, accountability, and data privacy are all included in these guidelines. Administrative structures plan to guarantee that artificial intelligence advancements line up with cultural qualities and stick to moral norms.

The European Association's Overall Information Security Guideline (GDPR) addresses a huge move toward tending to information protection concerns, influencing man-made intelligence applications that include individual information. Comparable drives overall are arising, stressing the requirement for capable artificial intelligence advancement.

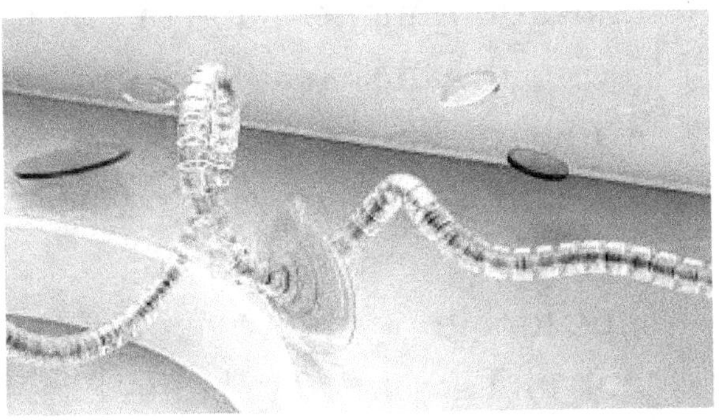

Industry-explicit norms and best practices are likewise developing. Cooperation between innovation organizations, policymakers, and backing bunches is fundamental to make far reaching structures that advance the capable utilization of man-made intelligence.

In the ensuing segments of this aide, we will dig into ten future dreams of artificial intelligence, each offering a one of a kind point of view on how this groundbreaking innovation might shape our reality. These dreams feature the likely headways and advantages as well as highlight the significance of moral contemplations and dependable improvement in controlling simulated intelligence towards a positive future.

Vision 1: The quest for General Artificial Intelligence

(AGI) is an ambitious goal in the field of artificial intelligence. It is leading the way toward the cognitive frontier. Dissimilar to tight or particular computer based intelligence frameworks intended for explicit errands, AGI tries to saturate machines with human-like mental capacities, empowering them to comprehend, learn, and apply information across an expansive range of spaces.

With this vision, AI research ventures into uncharted territory and faces formidable obstacles as well as thrilling opportunities.

4.1 Figuring out AGI

AGI, frequently alluded to areas of strength for as or full simulated intelligence, imagines machines with the ability to grasp the world in a way similar to human knowledge. These frameworks wouldn't be bound to single assignments yet rather have the capacity to move information across assorted areas, sum up data, and adjust to new circumstances with negligible direction.

The vital differentiator among AGI and current artificial intelligence frameworks lies in the extent of materialness. While contemporary computer based intelligence succeeds in unambiguous errands, AGI holds back nothing comprehension of the world, reflecting the mental adaptability and flexibility inborn in human knowledge.

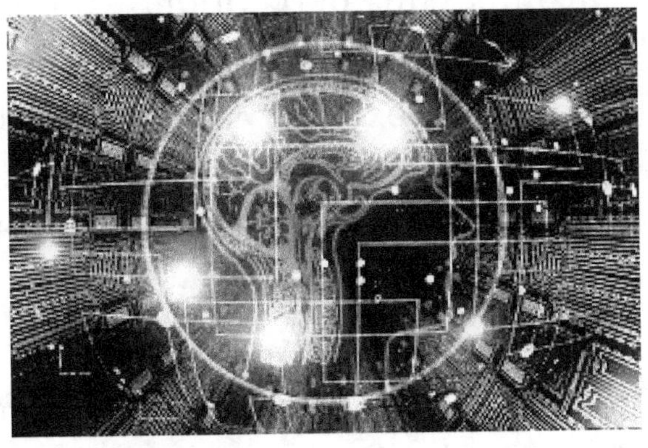

4.2 Difficulties and Potential outcomes

Acknowledging AGI presents significant specialized difficulties. Impersonating the intricacy of human discernment includes understanding conceptual ideas, good judgment thinking, and the capacity to gain from a great many encounters. Current computer based intelligence models, frequently advanced for limited errands, battle with such all encompassing perception.

The issue extends to AGI-related ethical considerations. Guaranteeing that AGI frameworks line up with human qualities, keep away from unsafe ways of behaving, and regard moral standards becomes basic. The expected effect on work, financial designs, and the moral treatment of AGI frameworks themselves bring up issues that request cautious thought.

In any case, the conceivable outcomes inborn in accomplishing AGI are extraordinary. Scientific discovery, resource management, and the development of solutions to complex global problems could all be revolutionized by such systems. The cooperative collaboration among people and AGI could open exceptional progressions in fields going from medication to space investigation.

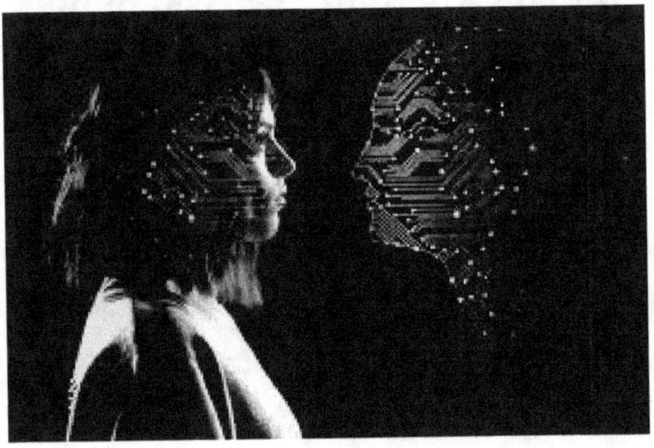

4.3 Effect on Society and Economy

The acknowledgment of AGI could reshape the structure holding the system together and the worldwide economy. The mix of AGI into different areas could prompt remarkable degrees of effectiveness, advancement, and critical thinking capacities. Ventures going from medical care and instruction to assembling and exploration could encounter significant changes.

All the while, the appearance of AGI raises financial worries. The possible uprooting of specific positions, changes in business elements, and the requirement for re-skilling the labor force become basic contemplations. Finding some kind of harmony between the advantages of AGI and the potential cultural interruptions requires cautious preparation and cooperation.

Administration structures and moral rules are fundamental in exploring the effect of AGI on society. Guaranteeing that AGI improvement sticks to standards of straightforwardness, responsibility, and reasonableness becomes critical in encouraging a future where AGI contributes emphatically to human government assistance.

In the ensuing segments of this aide, we will investigate nine additional dreams of man-made intelligence, each introducing a particular point of view on the future direction of computerized reasoning. As we dig further into these dreams, we will uncover the diverse scene that computer based intelligence is ready to cross, with AGI remaining as both an optimistic zenith and a subject of perplexing moral and specialized contemplations.

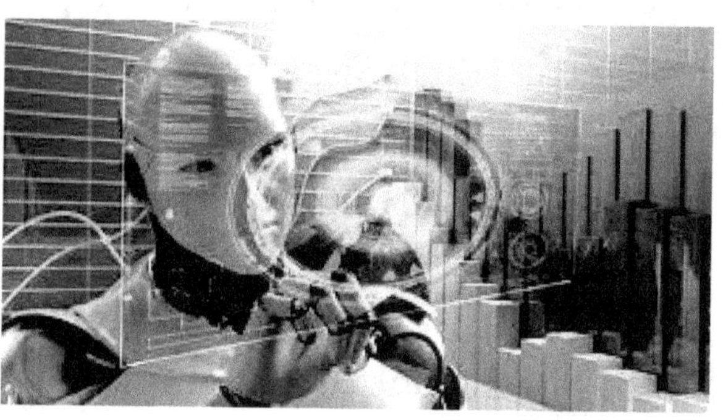

Vision 2: Human-Expanded Insight - Releasing Collaboration for Progress

In the domain of man-made reasoning, the vision of Human-Expanded Knowledge (HAI) marks a change in perspective that underscores coordinated effort among people and wise machines. Dissimilar to situations imagining machines as independent elements, HAI endeavors to upgrade human capacities, cultivating a future where computer based intelligence increases, instead of replaces, human insight. This vision reveals a scene where the cooperative energy between human instinct and simulated intelligence driven accuracy impels development and critical thinking to phenomenal levels.

5.1 Joint effort among simulated intelligence and People

Human-Expanded Knowledge imagines a cooperative relationship where man-made intelligence frameworks supplement human qualities and make up for limits. This collaborative strategy acknowledges that humans bring creativity, intuition, and ethical reasoning to the table, whereas AI excels at processing vast datasets, pattern recognition, and executing repetitive tasks.

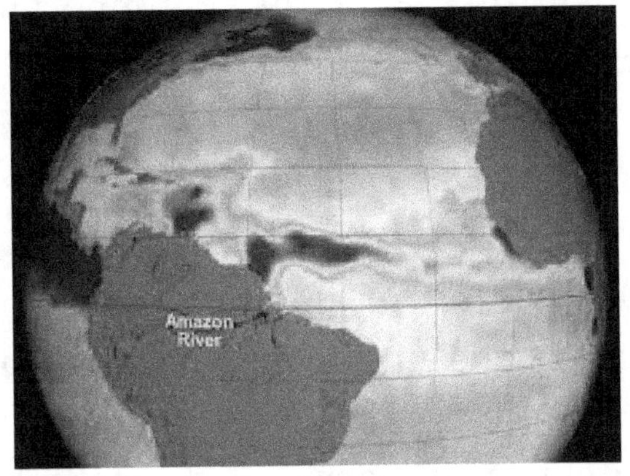

In down to earth terms, this cooperation could appear in man-made intelligence frameworks helping experts in different fields, like medical care, research, and imaginative undertakings. For example, in clinical diagnostics, computer based intelligence can break down complex clinical pictures to help specialists in precise and quick determinations. In research, artificial intelligence can filter through gigantic datasets to reveal designs, furnishing scientists with important experiences.

5.2 Upgrading Human Capacities

One of the focal fundamentals of HAI is the improvement of human capacities through man-made intelligence driven innovations. This incorporates a range of conceivable outcomes, including mental expansion, actual increase, and customized opportunities for growth.

Mental increase includes utilizing man-made intelligence to improve human mental capabilities, for example, memory, critical thinking, and direction. Savvy collaborators, fueled by computer based intelligence, can go about as mental expansions, giving constant data and investigation to expand human dynamic cycles.

The application of AI-driven technologies to enhance human physical capabilities is known as physical augmentation. This could go from exoskeletons that help with actual assignments to cerebrum machine interfaces that empower direct correspondence between the human mind and outside gadgets.

AI facilitates individualized learning experiences that cater to individual learning styles and preferences. Versatile learning stages can alter instructive substance, pacing, and evaluation techniques, guaranteeing that every student gets custom-made help for ideal understanding and ability improvement.

5.3 Possible Applications

The possible utilizations of Human-Expanded Knowledge range across different spaces:

Healthcare: Simulated intelligence helped diagnostics, customized therapy plans, and virtual wellbeing partners can change patient consideration and clinical direction.

Development and Research: Simulated intelligence can speed up logical disclosures by breaking down immense datasets, recognizing designs, and proposing speculations for additional examination.

Education: Versatile learning stages, smart coaching frameworks, and instructive chatbots can change the opportunity for growth, taking special care of individual requirements and encouraging a more profound comprehension of subjects.

Imagination and Plan: Artificial intelligence apparatuses can help imaginative experts by producing thoughts, aiding configuration cycles, and even co-making workmanship, music, or writing.

Proficient Administrations: Computer based intelligence fueled remote helpers can smooth out managerial errands, information investigation, and data recovery, permitting experts to zero in on additional key and imaginative parts of their work.

While HAI holds huge commitment, it likewise presents moral contemplations. To ensure that the enhancement of human intelligence is compatible with ethical principles, concerns regarding data privacy, accountability, and the possibility of bias in AI systems need to be carefully addressed.

As we venture through the different dreams of simulated intelligence, Human-Expanded Insight remains as a demonstration of the potential for cooperative energy between human creativity and man-made brainpower. The resulting areas will divulge extra points of view on the fate of computer based intelligence, each adding to the rich woven artwork of potential outcomes that this groundbreaking field holds.

Vision 3: Moral man-made intelligence and Mindful Turn of events - Exploring the Ethical Objective

In a period where Man-made brainpower (man-made intelligence) progressively shapes the structure holding the system together, the vision of Moral computer based intelligence and Mindful Improvement arises as an ethical compass directing the direction of man-made intelligence applications. This vision perceives the significant effect that simulated intelligence frameworks can have on people and networks, featuring the significance of moral contemplations, straightforwardness, and responsibility in the plan, sending, and administration of artificial intelligence advancements.

6.1 Guaranteeing Inclination Free Calculations

Tending to inclinations inside simulated intelligence calculations is a foundation of Moral computer based intelligence. Predisposition can accidentally be imbued in computer based intelligence frameworks through one-sided preparing information or unexpected algorithmic plan decisions. Guaranteeing that simulated intelligence applications are fair and impartial requires a coordinated work to distinguish and correct inclinations at each transformative phase.

Systems incorporate broadening preparing datasets, carrying out decency mindful calculations, and cultivating interdisciplinary coordinated efforts between ethicists, social researchers, and artificial intelligence engineers. The point is to make simulated intelligence frameworks that abstain from building up existing predispositions as well as effectively add to diminishing cultural variations.

6.2 Straightforwardness and Responsibility

Straightforwardness is a vital principle of Moral simulated intelligence, underscoring the requirement for clear and justifiable computer based intelligence frameworks. Clients and partners ought to have bits of knowledge into how simulated intelligence calculations decide, particularly when those choices influence people's lives. Straightforward man-made intelligence constructs trust as well as works with responsibility.

Engineers are urged to take on straightforward plan rehearses, record dynamic cycles, and convey the impediments of computer based intelligence frameworks. Laying out responsibility components guarantees that when issues emerge, people in question can be held liable, encouraging a culture of moral obligation inside the man-made intelligence local area.

6.3 Tending to Cultural Worries

Computer based intelligence's effect on society stretches out past specialized contemplations to include more extensive cultural worries. Moral computer based intelligence looks to resolve issues like work relocation, financial disparity, and the expected abuse of artificial intelligence innovations. Dependable advancement includes effectively captivating with these worries and pursuing arrangements that focus on cultural prosperity.

Drawing in with assorted partners, including local area delegates, policymakers, and promotion gatherings, helps in figuring out the shifted viewpoints and possible results of man-made intelligence applications. By encouraging comprehensive and participatory methodologies, Moral simulated intelligence plans to explore the perplexing transaction among innovation and society.

The vision of Moral computer based intelligence and Dependable Improvement isn't simply a hypothetical system; it requires substantial activities and joint efforts. As man-made intelligence keeps on advancing, moral contemplations should be essential to the improvement interaction. Finding some kind of harmony among development and moral standards guarantees that simulated intelligence advancements contribute emphatically to mankind without sustaining mischief or disparity.

We will examine additional AI visions in the following sections of this guide, each offering a distinct perspective on the technology's future. From medical services headways to ecological maintainability, every vision adds to a comprehensive comprehension of the potential and difficulties that lie ahead.

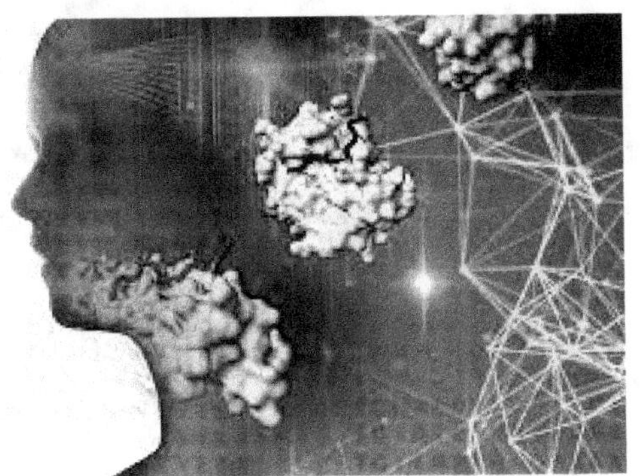

Vision 4: Simulated intelligence in Medical services - Changing Finding, Therapy, and Then some

The vision of simulated intelligence in Medical services connotes a progressive worldview, promising to reclassify the scene of clinical practices, diagnostics, and patient consideration. This vision imagines the consistent joining of man-made reasoning into medical care frameworks, with the possibility to upgrade exactness, proficiency, and availability across different clinical areas.

7.1 Customized Medication

One of the groundbreaking parts of man-made intelligence in Medical care is the coming of customized medication. Simulated intelligence calculations can examine huge datasets, including hereditary data, to fit clinical medicines to individual patients. This method optimizes treatment plans for improved outcomes and reduced side effects by taking into account genetic variations, lifestyle factors, and other nuances.

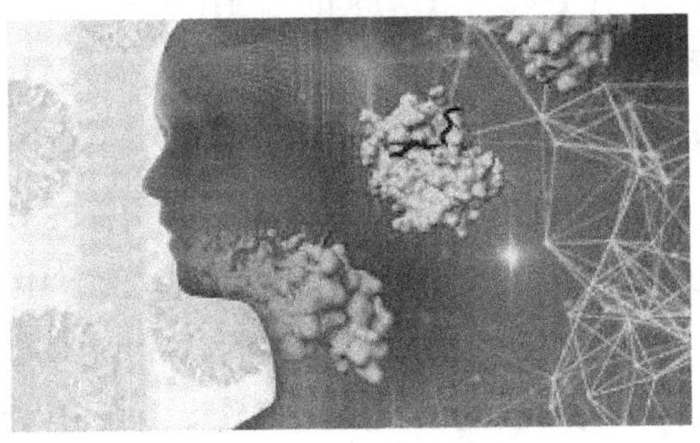

AI can assist in identifying specific genetic mutations that drive tumor growth, expanding the scope of precision medicine's potential application to cancer treatment. By understanding the exceptional hereditary profile of a patient's disease, clinicians can recommend designated treatments with higher viability.

7.2 Illness Forecast and Counteraction

Simulated intelligence's scientific capacities sparkle in sickness expectation and avoidance. Data from patients, such as medical records and diagnostic images, can be analyzed by machine learning models to discover patterns that may indicate health issues. Early recognition of infections like diabetes, cardiovascular circumstances, and neurodegenerative problems turns out to be more attainable, empowering opportune mediations and preventive measures.

In preventive medical services, man-made intelligence driven applications can evaluate a singular's gamble factors in view of different boundaries, presenting customized proposals for way of life adjustments, screenings, and immunizations. This proactive methodology holds the possibility to alleviate the beginning and movement of persistent circumstances.

7.3 simulated intelligence helped Medical services Experts

Simulated intelligence expands the capacities of medical care experts, offering important help in diagnostics, navigation, and authoritative undertakings. In clinical imaging, artificial intelligence calculations succeed at recognizing anomalies in X-beams, X-rays, and CT examines, helping radiologists in distinguishing conditions like cancers or breaks with more prominent exactness and speed.

By analyzing patient data, medical literature, and treatment outcomes, clinical decision support systems powered by AI aid physicians in selecting the most effective treatment plans. This cooperative methodology among computer based intelligence and medical services experts improves demonstrative precision and guarantees that therapy regimens line up with the most recent clinical exploration.

The coordination of simulated intelligence into authoritative undertakings, like clinical record the board and charging, smoothes out medical services tasks. This productivity permits medical services experts to devote additional opportunity to patient consideration and diminishes the weight of managerial above.

In the ensuing segments, we will keep on investigating assorted dreams of man-made intelligence, each revealing insight into the likely changes and contemplations related with the future development of computerized reasoning.

Fifth Vision: Free Frameworks and Mechanical advancement - Starting another Time of Computerization

The vision of Free Frameworks and Mechanical development proclaims a future where sharp machines, fit with the assumption for free heading and genuine undertakings, pervade different features of our regular timetables. In this situation, mechanical innovation and independent structures change organizations, transportation, and administrations to uncommon degrees of effectiveness, wellbeing, and solace.

8.1 Self-Driving vehicle as well as carrying

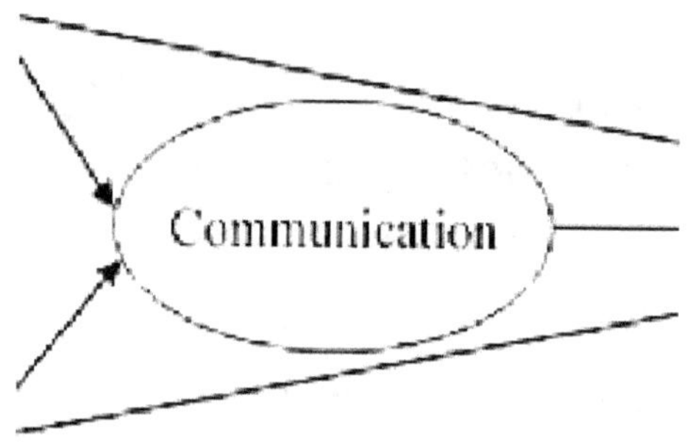

One of the most unmistakable appearances of Free Designs and Mechanical development is the movement of self-driving vehicles and sharp transportation frameworks. Vehicles can autonomously explore and go with choices on account of recreated knowledge estimations, which are upheld by sensors and continuous data taking care of abilities. The use of this advancement might conceivably reduce car accidents, redesign traffic stream, and lift by and large efficiency.

Notwithstanding confidential transportation, independent frameworks relax to cargo and strategies. Modernized development vehicles and robots furnished with man-made awareness driven course designs could maybe change the vehicle of things, further creating courses, diminishing vehicle times, and confining ordinary effect.

8.2 repeated information in Social affair

The joining of mechanical advancement and PC based

information in gathering processes watches out for a change of perspective in current mechanization. Sharp mechanical designs, outfitted with sensors and man-made reasoning limits, can adjust to dynamic conditions, perform different errands, and team up with human specialists dependably.

Sharp present day workplaces, driven through independent designs, can refresh creation work processes, expect support needs, and lessen spare energy. The final product is a more deft and talented get together climate that is reasonable for delivering excellent merchandise with expanded exactness and moderateness.

8.3 Hindrances and Entryways

No matter what the way that the vision of free structures and mechanical innovation opens up extra open doors, it moreover presents obstacles that require wary idea. To ensure the trustworthy association of free systems, it is critical for address security concerns, moral examinations, and the conceivable impact on work.

First and foremost, we must ensure the success of mechanized systems and autonomous vehicles. Serious testing, administrative plans, and shield instruments are fundamental bits of making solid independent frameworks. Moreover, in conditions where moral route is required, moral guidelines ought to be spread on a mission to control the approach to acting of free machines.

The potential for work relocation considering broadened mechanization is a social test related with this vision. In any case, it likewise brings significant entrances for the improvement of new situations in organizing, remaining mindful of, and managing free frameworks. To ensure a smooth advancement into the workforce, proactive measures like tutoring and it are principal to deskilling drives.

The vision of Independent Frameworks and Mechanical advancement holds the probability to upset associations, further foster transportation, and reconsider work. It is vital for offset improvement with moral contemplations to exploit the upsides of autonomous structures and examine the confusing issues they present.

As we plunge into the ensuing segments of this partner, every vision fans out as an uncommon region in the making story of modernized thinking, adding to the different winding of potential outcomes that what's in store.

Vision 6: PC based insight for Normal Acceptability - A Catalyst for Overall Insurance

The vision of computerized reasoning for Regular Legitimacy envisions a reality where man-made intellectual ability transforms into areas of strength for an intending to crushing natural challenges. This vision aims to improve asset across the board, monitor and alleviate environmental change, and cultivate manageable practices across various areas by addressing the scientific capability of computer-based intelligence.

9.1 Environment displaying and forecasting

Computer-based intelligence is a crucial tool in environment displaying and forecasting due to its ability to analyze vast and intricate datasets. This, hence, upholds expecting ridiculous environment events, seeing long stretch climate floats, and sorting out frameworks for climate adaptability.

By engrossing ceaseless data and certain examples, PC based insight adds to correct climate guaging. This is particularly critical for feeble regions leaned to disastrous occasions, enabling early reprimands and working with proactive measures to ease the impact on networks and natural frameworks.

9.2 Resource The board

Improving resource the board is essential to viable development, and mimicked knowledge brings a data driven method for managing this endeavor. In agriculture, man-made consciousness energized structures can take apart soil prosperity, crop conditions, and weather patterns to propel water framework, readiness, and vermin control. Accuracy agribusiness uses man-made intelligence to limit asset use, reduce environmental impact, and increase crop yields.

In water resource the board, recreated knowledge estimations can analyze data from sensors and satellites to screen water quality, expect droughts, and further develop water scattering. This helpers in ensuring sensible usage of water resources and lightening the impact of water lack.

9.3 The Role of Artificial Intelligence in Renewable

Energy Increasing the output and effectiveness of renewable energy sources requires the use of artificial intelligence. In sun fueled and wind energy, man-created knowledge computations can measure energy creation considering air conditions, enabling cross section overseers to change natural market as a matter of fact. Prescient support driven by man-made intelligence additionally makes environmentally friendly power foundation more dependable.

Through brilliant structures powered by simulated intelligence, energy efficiency in buildings and urban communities can be improved. From changing lighting and temperature considering inhabitance to expecting top energy interest, PC based insight adds to the progression of splendid, energy-capable circumstances.

While reenacted insight for Regular Practicality holds immense potential, moral considerations and careful course of action are essential. Discovering some sort of congruity among advancement and natural safeguarding ensures that man-made reasoning developments become stimuli for positive change as opposed to adding to negative aftereffects possibly.

Ecological supportability's vision of simulated intelligence reflects a commitment to using technology for the greater good. In this aid, we look at various visions of artificial intelligence and see how each one fits into the ongoing story of human resourcefulness overcoming obstacles posed by computerized reasoning.

7th Vision: Quantum Figuring and man-made intelligence - Releasing Extraordinary Computational Power

The vision of Quantum Figuring and man-made intelligence addresses a groundbreaking intermingling of two state of the art innovations, promising to reform the scene of computerized reasoning. This vision imagines the reconciliation of quantum figuring capacities with man-made intelligence calculations, opening phenomenal computational power and taking care of complicated issues that were once considered inconceivable for traditional PCs.

10.1 Outline of Quantum Registering

Quantum registering use the standards of quantum mechanics to perform calculations at a dramatic scale contrasted with traditional PCs. Quantum bits, or quits, which can exist in multiple states simultaneously, have taken the place of traditional bits. Quantum computers are able to process a lot of information and complete complex calculations for some problems much more quickly than classical computers because of this parallelism.

10.2 Quantum man-made intelligence and AI

The combination of quantum processing with simulated intelligence presents Quantum computer based intelligence, a worldview that investigates how quantum calculations can improve AI and enhancement undertakings. Quantum AI calculations influence the interesting properties of quits to process and break down huge datasets more productively than old style calculations.

Quantum calculations can possibly beat old style calculations in errands like enhancement, design acknowledgment, and tackling complex streamlining issues. This ability could have significant ramifications for enterprises going from money and strategies to sedate disclosure and materials science.

10.3 Ramifications for what's to come

The cooperative energy between Quantum Figuring and man-made intelligence holds the commitment of tending to difficulties that as of now outperform the abilities of traditional PCs. With quantum computing computational power, tasks like simulating molecular structures for drug discovery, optimizing complex systems, and breaking encryption algorithms become feasible.

In medical care, Quantum artificial intelligence could assist the course of medication revelation by mimicking sub-atomic associations with remarkable exactness. This could result in the development of novel diseases' treatments and therapies.

The monetary area stands to profit from the upgraded computational capacities of Quantum man-made intelligence, especially in advancing portfolios, risk evaluation, and extortion recognition. Quantum calculations could beat old style calculations in complex monetary demonstrating assignments.

Be that as it may, the combination of quantum figuring and computer based intelligence additionally presents critical specialized and pragmatic difficulties. Quantum PCs are as of now in their beginning stages, with viable, enormous scope quantum PCs still a work in progress. Conquering issues connected with mistake rates, adaptability, and keeping up with qubit soundness presents impressive obstacles that specialists and architects are effectively tending to.

Despite being futuristic, the vision of quantum computing and artificial intelligence highlights the potential for revolutionary developments at the intersection of quantum technology and AI. As these advancements experienced, the aggregate effect on computational capacities, critical thinking, and logical disclosure is ready to reclassify the limits of what is conceivable.

Vision 8: Computer based intelligence in Schooling - Customizing Learning Excursions

The vision of computer based intelligence in Schooling addresses an extraordinary way to deal with picking up, utilizing man-made brainpower to tailor instructive encounters, improve showing procedures, and give customized learning excursions to understudies. This vision imagines an instructive scene where man-made intelligence innovations enhance understudy commitment, support teachers, and encourage a more comprehensive and versatile learning climate.

11.1 Customized Learning Ways

One of the vital mainstays of simulated intelligence in Schooling is the idea of customized learning. Man-made intelligence calculations can dissect individual learning styles, inclinations, and execution information to tailor instructive substance and exercises. This approach guarantees that every understudy advances at their own speed, gets designated help in areas of trouble, and is tested fittingly in solid areas.

Versatile learning stages fueled by simulated intelligence can progressively change the trouble and content of examples in light of an understudy's reactions, advancing a more profound comprehension of subjects. This personalization stretches out past scholarly substance to incorporate contemplations for understudies' socio-close to home prosperity and individual interests.

11.2 Savvy Coaching Frameworks

Artificial intelligence assumes a vital part in the improvement of savvy coaching frameworks that offer individualized help to understudies. These frameworks can evaluate an understudy's assets and shortcomings, recognize confusions, and proposition continuous criticism and direction. Smart mentoring frameworks add to working on scholarly results by giving designated intercessions and encouraging a steady learning climate.

11.3 Computerizing Authoritative Errands

Computer based intelligence smoothes out authoritative errands in the schooling area, permitting teachers to zero in more on educating and tutoring. Chat bots and menial helpers can deal with routine regulatory questions, saving time for instructors to draw in with understudies, plan imaginative showing materials, and give customized consideration.

Managerial errands, like reviewing appraisals, can be robotized through man-made intelligence, giving speedy and predictable input to understudies. This recoveries time for teachers as well as empowers ideal bits of knowledge into understudy execution, considering brief mediations when required.

11.4 Inclusive Education and Accessibility

AI addresses accessibility issues to help make education more accessible to all students. For understudies with different advancing necessities, man-made intelligence controlled instruments can offer altered help, like text-to-discourse abilities, versatile points of interaction, and continuous language interpretation. This encourages a comprehensive learning climate where all understudies, no matter what their capacities, can effectively take an interest.

11.5 Difficulties and Moral Contemplations

While the vision of computer based intelligence in Training holds extraordinary commitment, it likewise presents difficulties and moral contemplations. Information protection, guaranteeing impartial calculations, and tending to the advanced separation are basic angles that request consideration. Transparent policies, ongoing algorithm evaluation, and a commitment to equal access to technological resources are necessary for the responsible implementation of AI in education.

As we explore the developing scene of man-made intelligence, the vision of computer based intelligence in Training arises as an impetus for change, opening the possibility to make connecting with, customized, and comprehensive growth opportunities for understudies all over the planet. In the ensuing areas of this aide, we will keep on investigating different dreams, each adding to the rich woven artwork of potential outcomes that man-made reasoning presents.

Vision 9: AI and innovation

A time when artificial intelligence will become a partner, a motivator, and a source of inspiration in the creative process is predicted by the vision of AI and Creativity. AI and innovation: An Agreeable Coordinated effort simulated intelligence is imagined as a device that improves imaginative articulation, works with development, and opens up new boondocks in fields like writing, plan, and music — not as a swap for human innovativeness.

12.1 Inventive Assistance and Inspiration

Reenacted insight computations are dynamically being used to help and energize creatives across various disciplines. In workmanship and plan, PC based knowledge devices can deliver visual thoughts, help the development of cutting edge craftsmanship, and even co-make with human trained professionals. This planned exertion develops the imaginative reach, giving new perspectives and possible results that probably won't have been considered anyway.

Artificial intelligence can decipher designs, deconstruct massive melodic datasets, and create one-of-a-kind pieces in music structure. Agreeable undertakings among craftsmen and PC based insight systems achieve intriguing and creative melodic pieces, showing the cooperation between human nature and machine-delivered imagination.

12.2 Further developing Arrangement and Improvement

PC based insight adds to setup processes through automating excess tasks, making plan assortments, and offering judicious pieces of information. In designing, for example, mimicked knowledge can propel structure plans for energy efficiency, essential reliability, and classy charm. Computer based intelligence and planners cooperate to take a gander at various potential outcomes and make the iterative plan process more straightforward.

Improvement is in like manner filled by man-made brainpower driven encounters. Associations impact man-made knowledge to separate market designs, purchaser lead, and emerging advances, coordinating imperative decisions and empowering a culture of steady turn of events. The limit of man-made knowledge to process and separate colossal proportions of data speeds up the conspicuous confirmation of cunning contemplations and game plans.

12.3 Describing and Content Creation

Man-made insight estimations are continuously drawn in with content creation and describing. The age of intelligent and logically important text is made possible by Regular Language Handling (NLP). Mimicked knowledge controlled catboats, virtual characters, and record age structures add to natural describing experiences in gaming and virtual circumstances.

In news inclusion, computerized reasoning guides content creation by looking at data, delivering reports, and regardless, offering encounters into expected reports. This participation grants journalists to focus in on scientific points while PC based knowledge handles routine tasks.

12.4 Moral Examinations

While the organized exertion among man-made brainpower and imaginativeness opens stimulating possible results, moral examinations ought to be tended to. Regard for protected innovation privileges, variety in preparing information to stay away from predispositions, and straightforwardness in attribution of man-made intelligence created content are urgent angles. Discovering some sort of agreement between creative extension and moral guidelines ensures that computerized reasoning in creative mind contributes decidedly to social verbalization.

Vision 10: The vision of the cultural effect of man-made intelligence

Looks at the more extensive outcomes, challenges, and amazing opportunities that the unlimited reception of computerized reasoning brings to networks, economies, and the structure that holds the system together. The vision of the cultural effect of man-made intelligence looks at the challenges and amazing opportunities. As mimicked insight headways continue to create, this vision researches the huge repercussions on business, ethics, organization, and the scattering of benefits and risks across various sections of society.

13.1 Employment Dynamics

The incorporation of AI has an impact on the employment dynamics of various industries and sectors. Computerization driven by reproduced knowledge could provoke the dislodging of explicit positions, particularly those including standard, terrible tasks. Simultaneously, it opens up new open doors in simulated intelligence advancement, upkeep, and oversight.

Tries to address potential work removing incorporate techniques, for instance, reskilling and upskilling the workforce to acclimate to the changing position scene. Tutoring and getting ready drives expect an essential part in arranging individuals for occupations that enhancement and collaborate with man-made knowledge developments.

13.2 Contemplations of Morality

The cultural impact of artificial intelligence raises significant moral questions. Predictability in simulated intelligence calculations, simplicity in dynamic cycles, and the effective application of advancements in artificial intelligence are primary concerns. Ensuring goodness, obligation, and the security of individual honors and assurance become essential in the development and sending of PC based knowledge systems.

Reenacted knowledge systems affecting fundamental locales like policing, administrations, and cash demand mindful assessment to swear off proliferating or demolishing existing social inclinations. Mindful artificial intelligence sending requires the foundation of moral rules, different portrayal in artificial intelligence improvement groups, and continuous assessments of algorithmic reasonableness.

13.3 Organization and Rule

The creating scene of man-made knowledge prompts the prerequisite for fruitful organization and rule. Policymakers, industry trailblazers, and experts collaborate to spread out structures that offset headway with moral considerations and social success. Rules wrap districts like data security, algorithmic obligation, and the ethical use of mimicked knowledge in delicate spaces.

Overall joint exertion is fundamental in watching out for the overall thought of PC based knowledge challenges. Guidelines and standards are orchestrated to ensure a robust and capable approach to simulated intelligence development and international transmission.

13.4 Effect on the Economy

Man-made brainpower meaningfully affects the economy too, influencing imbalance, admittance to innovation, and pay dispersion. A far reaching understanding of the likely advantages and risks of computer based intelligence innovations is important for exploring these impacts.

Drives to increase inclusivity, guarantee equal access to educational resources, and build the computerized partition are all efforts to reduce financial disparities. Social techniques and money related methods that consider the repercussions of recreated insight add to a more impartial dissemination of benefits.

13.5 Changing Turn of events and Rule

The vision of the social impact of man-made reasoning features the touchy congruity between developing turn of events and doing strong rule. Technologists, policymakers, and the wider community must continuously collaborate to embrace artificial intelligence's groundbreaking capabilities while protecting cultural values.

Considering everything, the social impact of PC based insight is dynamic, multifaceted, and constantly progressing. The aggregate endeavors of society will assume a pivotal part in forming a future wherein simulated intelligence contributes emphatically to the prosperity of mankind as we explore the difficulties and open doors introduced by simulated intelligence. The more extensive account of simulated intelligence's process is caught in this last vision, which underlines the meaning of capable turn of events and smart combination into our social orders.

Conclusion: Exploring the Future Scene of Man-made brainpower

As we close this investigation of ten visionary viewpoints on the fate of man-made consciousness, it becomes obvious that computer based intelligence is an extraordinary power with the possibility to reshape essentially every part of our lives. Every vision offers a special focal point through which we can expect the development of computer based intelligence and its effect on different spaces, from medical services and schooling to innovativeness and cultural designs.

The direction of man-made intelligence is definitely not a straight way however a perplexing and dynamic excursion, set apart by difficulties, potential open doors, and moral contemplations. The dreams introduced highlight the requirement for mindful turn of events, insightful administration, and a faithful obligation to guaranteeing that simulated intelligence innovations line up with human qualities and contribute decidedly to society.

From the quest for General Computerized reasoning (AGI) and Human-Expanded Knowledge to the coordination of artificial intelligence in medical care, ecological maintainability, and imaginative undertakings, the dreams on the whole paint a rich embroidery of potential outcomes. The approach of Quantum Registering and the cooperative collaboration among simulated intelligence and inventiveness feature the imaginative wildernesses that lie ahead.

Moral contemplations pervade each feature of man-made intelligence advancement, from addressing inclinations and guaranteeing straightforwardness to exploring the financial effect and laying out hearty administration systems. The dreams stress the significance of inclusivity, reasonableness, and impartial dispersion of advantages as we tackle the capability of computer based intelligence.

In this period of fast mechanical progression, the joint effort among people and computer based intelligence remains as a common topic. Whether it's the expansion of human knowledge, the advantageous interaction between imaginative undertakings and man-made intelligence help, or the conjunction in a general public impacted via independent frameworks, these dreams highlight the potential for amicable cooperation.

As we explore the future scene of man-made intelligence, it is critical to stay cautious, versatile, and focused on cultivating a climate where development lines up with moral standards. The dreams introduced in this guide are not foreordained results but rather plans that welcome aggregate cooperation in molding a future where man-made consciousness improves the human experience and adds to the advancement of society. The journey goes on, and the conversation about AI's future continues to be an open and changing story that is shaped by our choices today.